THE GIFT OF LOVE

Other Writings of Joel S. Goldsmith

The Gift of Love

Joel S. Goldsmith

Edited By
Lorraine Sinkler

I-Level Publications
Publishers

Lakewood, CO   ❦   Austell, GA

Published by *I*-Level Publications under a reprint arrangement with
HarperCollins Publishers. All rights reserved.
I-Level Publications is an imprint of Acropolis Books, Inc.
Printed in the United States of America.

I-Level Publications
747 Sheridan Blvd., Suite 1A, Lakewood, Colorado 80214-2551
or
6558 Dunwoody Trail, Austell, Georgia 30001-5325
http://www.i-level.com

LIBRARY OF CONGRESS CATALOGING-IN-PUBLICATION DATA

Goldsmith, Joel S. , 1892–1964.
    The gift of love / Joel S. Goldsmith ; edited by Lorraine Sinkler.
        p.   cm.
    Originally published: New York : Harper & Row, 1975.
    Includes bibliographical references.
    ISBN 1-889051-10-1 (alk. paper)
    1. Love—Religious aspects—Christianity.   2. Spiritual life–
    –Christianity.   I. Sinkler, Lorraine.   II. Title.
[BV4639.G65 1996]
299' .93—dc20   96-41968
                                                                   CIP

THIS BOOK IS PRINTED ON ACID FREE PAPER THAT MEETS STANDARD Z 39.48 OF
THE AMERICAN NATIONAL STANDARDS INSTITUTE

Except the Lord build the house,
they labour in vain that build it.

—Psalm 127

"Illumination dissolves all material ties and binds
men together with the golden chains of spiritual
understanding; it acknowledges only the leadership
of the Christ; it has no ritual or rule but the divine,
impersonal universal Love; no other worship than
the inner Flame that is ever lit at the shrine of
Spirit. This union is the free state of spiritual broth-
erhood. The only restraint is the discipline of Soul;
therefore, we know liberty without license; we are
a united universe without physical limits, a divine
service to God without ceremony or creed. The
illumined walk without fear—by Grace."

—*The Infinite Way* by Joel S. Goldsmith

PUBLISHER'S
PREFACE

Simple, yet profound; brief yet complete; impersonal yet loving. These are descriptions that best identify, but differentiate the work of Joel Goldsmith from other mystics of the twentieth century. This becomes particularly apparent in *The Gift of Love*.

Most mystics will agree that as sentimental as the term love has become, this is really the only word that describes the individual's outlook toward all existence once he has entered the fourth dimensional state of consciousness. Love is often used as a noun, as an alternative for the name of God, representing the only power flowing through all things to accomplish its own ends. Joel Goldsmith, however, in his realization of the Omnipresence, Omnipotence and Omniscience of God sees love as a verb: this very state of consciousness flowing through all life.

Joel Goldsmith did not see himself as a loving individual. Yet everyone that became part of his universe and orbit found him to be extremely loving, but on an impersonal level. He looked at each individual as an expression of eternal Oneness; and in that realization, felt a love toward each person that transcended any concept of the term from a human standpoint. This in fact was, according to Goldsmith, the healing consciousness that could impersonalize and nothingize the appearance, looking through it to the reality that lies at the foundation of every appearance. He never saw an individual as being good or bad. These terms merely represented a distorted and unenlightened understanding of the true nature of each individual. When one could see this judgment of good and bad as simply representing a concept of this world and having no power, love naturally flowed forth and healings were obvious and abundant.

Joel Goldsmith felt every one of us were transparencies of love and that love, in its unconditioned and free flowing nature, looked through the three dimensional human appearance and saw every neighbor, friend, family member and enemy as the same beautiful expression of God. This is the vision of the mystic and this was reality to Goldsmith.

In its continuing commitment to provide mystical literature at the highest level of consciousness, *I*-Level Publications is pleased to present *The Gift of Love* as a compact but essential representation of this mystic's realization on the subject of love expressing the depth of consciousness attained by him.

We remain grateful that this material is available and are committed to make additional works of Joel Goldsmith increasingly available to a world in search of answers.

– *I*-Level Publications

TABLE OF CONTENTS

TABLE OF CONTENTS

~ 1 ~

LOVE
AS
UNDERSTANDING

We all want to be understood and to be understanding. Most of us wish that those we meet could see into the center of our being, could see what we have been from the beginning, but which no one has yet recognized—not mother, not father, not teacher. No one has ever seen what we really are, and it is because of this nonrecognition that we have worn a mask to hide ourselves from the world.

If only the mask that is hiding you from me and me from you could drop from our faces, we would be like children, back in the Garden of Eden.

Everyone longs to be understood, but most persons think that that means being known as they are humanly. That is not what it means at all. Those who believe that do so because they do not yet know that the Christ is their true identity and this is really what they would like to show forth.

The Master Christ Jesus, too, longed to have his true identity recognized and understood. How obvious is his longing as he asks, "Whom do men say that I the Son of man am? . . . Whom say ye that I am?" He longed to be known as the Christ, but he could not walk out and say, "I am the Christ."

Let us not hesitate, however, to say silently and secretly to everyone we meet, "Thou art the Christ, the holy one of Israel. I know thee who thou art." How do we know it? Flesh and blood have not taught us this, nor has the human mind revealed it. Only spiritual discernment reveals to us that God lives on earth as individual you and me. God has incarnated Himself as individual being. God the Father appears on earth as God the son.

As we begin the practice of beholding the Christ in everyone we meet—in our household, our neighborhood, the market, the post office, the department store—the world will begin to present a different picture to us. People will act in a different way. The world will respond differently to us because the world will bring back to us what we have given to it.

Whomever we meet, we meet in the spirit of letting God's grace flow through us. Wherever we go, we go in a giving spirit. This does not necessarily imply giving of our personal possessions or giving of our time and effort, although some of that may be involved also. The greater giving is the recognition of the true identity of those we meet: "I know thee who thou art, the holy one of Israel."

Everyone is the holy one of Israel. Every saint and every devil is that holy one. Every healthy person, every diseased person, every pure person, every sinning person is the holy one of Israel, God incarnate, although temporarily acting out the part of the Prodigal Son, or the branch of a tree that is cut off.

To enrich our own life we must learn to give recognition to the true identity of those we meet. The person we meet today is presenting his Christhood for identification. He thinks he is presenting a sick body to be healed, a disturbed mind to be set at peace, an empty purse to be filled, or morals to be cleansed. But we know better.

We do not claim that a person's human form and characteristics are the Christ. No person in his human identity is spiritual, perfect, healthy, or wealthy. But we disregard the appearance of his humanhood and through spiritual discernment behold the Christ looking out of his eyes silently, sacredly, secretly.

We see him from the mystical standpoint after the manner of the Christ, knowing that whoever he is, he is presenting his Christhood for our acknowledgment. We may be faced with a gambler, a prostitute, a sick or a dying person, but always he is presenting his Christhood to us for recognition and identification.

Every time some person comes to us trying to convince us that he has a sick body, an empty purse, or is living a sinful life, we learn not to try to change the evil into good, not to pray that God take away the negative appearance and restore the positive. Rather, we ignore the appearance, look right through it, and see that behind the eyes of every individual is the Christ.

That is what Jesus saw when he looked into the eyes of the woman taken in adultery. He

saw her begging and pleading to be known as
she really was and not as she appeared to be.
The thief on the cross was begging to be recognized: "Look, I am a thief; I did steal, but you
know me better than that. You know it was
only because I thought I needed something.
You know who I am; you know what I am."

And the Master looked right into his eyes, "I
will take you, not your body, but you whom I
see behind the eyes, I will take that right into
paradise with me this moment—not after pun-
ishment, no, this moment. If your sins are
scarlet, you are white as snow."

Are we white as snow? No, not our
humanhood that has sinned. But as the holy
one of Israel, I^* have never sinned. I is the
Christ of God; I is God incarnate as individual
being. As we behold that Christ in any person,
in some measure at least he is healed of his
humanhood and of all finite limitation, and as
he beholds that in us, we, too, are lifted up.

---

*I, italicized, refers to God.

Enter into the sanctuary of your own being, and there in silence and secrecy behold the true identity of friend or foe. Lift up the son of God in him to your level, knowing that the Christ of him is the Christ of you.

~2~

LIVING
BY
LOVE

To be obedient to the law of love brings us into the kingdom of God. But what does that obedience entail? It is a service to God through service to man. It is being obedient to the command to pray for our enemies, to forgive those who persecute or otherwise ill-treat us. No one can serve God except in loving service to man because there is no God separate and apart from man. All the God there is, is made manifest on earth as man, and inasmuch as we do that service unto man, we do it unto God. Believing that we can serve God and ignore man is blindness.

The only truly spiritual life possible is lived by keeping our thoughts and deeds in at-one-ment with the law of love—not a sentimental, emotional kind of love, not a nonsensical, wishy-washy kind of love. It must be the love that does unto others as we would have them do unto us. That is all there is to real love.

The only trouble is that love has been confused with sentiment. People have become all worked up into a state of emotionalism, believing that emotionalism has something to do with love while all the time they were not fulfilling the terms of love.

Love is not a sentimental attachment to mankind: love is a law; love is a mode of conduct, an attitude. Love does not come to us. Love is within ourselves, and we must open out a way for it to escape by fulfilling the commands of the Master. Love is something that we let flow out from us, just as we open a way for truth to flow out from us.

It is we ourselves, however, who must know whether or not we are functioning through love. At this point egotism and conceit could come in and cheat us by developing within us a pharisaical self-righteousness. We have to be careful that we do not get the idea that we, of ourselves, are loving. We must realize that it is the love of God that enables us to be loving, God's love, not our love, and not even our love for God.

Instead let us think of it as God's love for us: "God so loved the world, that he gave his only begotten Son"—to each one of us individually. At the very center of our being God has incarnated Himself in us as His son. God the Father has placed Himself as God the Son in the

midst of us. That means every person who has
ever existed since the beginning of time or
who ever will exist. Every person has the seed
of Godhood at his center. God so loved mankind that He placed Himself in the midst of
mankind. He placed the individual expression
of Himself at the center of us and He named
that center *I*. He named Himself *I*, and every
time the word *I* comes to our consciousness we
should realize that the presence of God is
there.

We have to maintain ourselves consciously
in the awareness that the son of God is in us
and Its law is love. We are in attunement with
It when we are doing unto others as we would
have them do unto us, when we are forgiving
"seventy times seven," when we are sharing,
giving, bestowing.

The law of God is forgiveness and doing
unto others as we would have others do unto
us. We are violating the law of love the moment

we desire revenge, indulge in resentment, or ascribe wrong motives to anyone. Every person is in attunement with the law of love when he is living according to his highest light of doing unto others as he would have others do unto him.

"Inasmuch as ye did it not to one of the least of these, ye did it not to me," for the only "me" there is, is man; the only God there is, is the incarnation of Himself in man. When we are serving and recognizing the God in man, we are serving and recognizing the only true God.

~ 3 ~

LOVE
THY
NEIGHBOR

❧

In order to love our neighbor as ourselves, we have to move out of the human sense of love into the Divine. To be very honest, not many persons are really able to love human beings. The ones we do love supremely and those in whom we put our faith and trust sometimes fail us. To love our neighbor as ourselves, therefore, does not mean that we are to love the human race with all its failings.

This would not be loving our neighbor as ourselves. This would be being blind.

When I look at a person, I must not look at his outer human appearance and love that. I must look through him and realize that in the midst of him God is, and that God is living his life. I see in him the image and likeness of God, the presence of God, the glory of God. If I accepted what I see with my eyes, I would be disappointed in far too many persons. But I look through the appearance they present and acknowledge:

In you is the child of God; in you dwells the Christ of God. In your true being, God is your life, God is your soul, God is your mind.

It does not matter how evil the person may appear to be. I look through that to the divinity which is at the center of his being and say to myself, "I love you as I love my Self, because my Self is your Self. God's Self is my Self and God's Self is your Self. There is only one spiritual Self."

In this way I am crediting God with having given expression only to His own spiritual image and likeness which is forever perfect, and I love that image and likeness as my Self. I find nothing in him to forgive, because I see nothing in him but his spiritual selfhood. I find nothing in him to excuse, nothing to judge, nothing to criticize, nothing to condemn. I am not dealing with a human being: I am dealing with the image and likeness of God which is his true selfhood.

As we love God and our neighbor in this way, we remove ourselves from the human sense of law and bring ourselves under Grace. As long as I hold a person under the law of humanhood, that law is operating in my experience. The moment I remove him from the law and see him under Grace, I am myself under Grace. In releasing him, I have released myself because there is only one of us, not two.

Once I have released a person from his humanhood and have loved him as I would have him love me, the law no longer operates. If I look through his eyes and see the Christ of him, how can I wrong him? I have lost my capacity and my desire to wrong him because I see him now as the spiritual image and likeness of God. And how could I harm the child of God?

Is it not clear that I have released myself from the law because now I do not have to do good to him and I cannot do evil to him? I can see him only as he is, and this is loving him as myself. I know myself to be spiritual, the child of God. I know that I am one with the Father and I know that the Father is always saying, "Son, thou art ever with me, and all that I have is thine." All I am doing is realizing the same thing for him and seeing him in the same light.

When I see a person in this light, I am loving him spiritually, and I have released him from the law of good and evil. In releasing him, I have released myself. I have released him into his spiritual relationship with God, but in doing that I have done it also unto myself because there is but one Self. After that I have lost the capacity to do a person any injury or wrong; but I have also lost the capacity to do any good because now I am that place where God shines through.

"My peace I give unto you: not as the world giveth." Wherever we go, whether in the office, at the market, or in our home we take that peace into our consciousness and carry it with us throughout the day. Wherever we go we carry this message silently and secretly, "My peace I give unto you," the Christ-peace. Then we can witness how within a few days people begin to change their attitude toward us. We are releasing the Christ, and those toward whom It is released cannot help but feel It. As we go out into the world, carrying that one message, "My peace give I unto thee, God's grace give I unto thee, the peace that passes understanding give I unto thee, the Christ-peace, the spiritual peace," we are bound to meet with a response.

As we make a practice of doing this no matter where we go, as we learn to let that flow out from the *I* of our being, everyone who comes in contact with us will know that we are blessing him. He will not know how nor understand, but he will think he has met up with a pleasant and agreeable person; he will feel something.

True, there are 10 or 20 percent so adamant in their humanhood that we could love them intensely and they would not even know it. But between 80 and 90 percent of all the people in the world are receptive and responsive to spiritual truth, and if we are living in the atmosphere of "My peace give I unto thee," "God's grace be unto thee," they will respond.

In doing this we have kept truth active in our consciousness; we have spent divine love. We have cast our bread upon the waters, and that is what is going to come back to us. But if in our ignorance we are looking for good to come to us, or if we are seeking to demonstrate good, we are outside the spiritual way of life because we are failing to recognize the already infinite nature of our being.

not because we have gained what we

but because we have found our h

bosom.

Since only God can tab

is only when you

humanhood into a

that we can m

that God

fusing

un

th

a de

there is

known eac

time evolves, th

common: music, li

life is lived as one inst

The same relationship

higher plane when we come

God. We have met our own; we

23

~4~

OUR LOVE FOR GOD

Thou shalt love the Lord thy God with all thine heart, and with all thy soul, and with all thy might.

Deuteronomy 6:5

That is a command. But how many persons are there in the world who feel a real love for God? Love, itself, is somewhat of an abstraction, and certainly to love an unknown or invisible God does not bring forth a very tangible or warm feeling.

Eventually, however, there must come into individual consciousness a love for God that is deeper than any love that a human being has ever known. That cannot come about if we persist in thinking of God as an impersonal principle, an impersonal law, or an impersonal life. True, God is all that, but God is more than that. To me, God is very personal. T[...] said that God is "closer . . . than br[...] nearer than hands and feet." S[...] thinking of anything as col[...] as impersonal as mus[...] warmth that was [...] personal prese[...] The lo[...] comes [...] wh[...]

own self in another form; we have met our own state of being. Then comes a communion, as personal a communion as friends can ever know. In that communion, ultimately there is the realization that we have nothing of ourselves, that whatever we have of love, wisdom, guidance, or direction is really of the Father, and what we have or use is actually the capacity and the ability of the Father, rather than our own.

It would seem in those moments as if there were an interchange, as if there were something flowing from the person to God, and then flowing back from God to the person. It may seem difficult to believe that God could need anything that we have. Probably it is not that God needs anything, but rather that since we are one with the Father, that which is of the Father and which flows to the son is likewise flowing back from the son to the Father in the same way that love passes from the parent to the child, and then returns to the parent.

There is a height that is sometimes reached when the personal self disappears and nothing is left but God. That is a rare experience in anyone's life. Some have known it only once in a lifetime; some have known it two, three, or four times. Some few can enter into the relationship almost at will. It is a rare thing, but accounts of that experience can be found in those passages of mystical literature where the mystic describes himself as the life of the blade of grass, the life of the flower, or the life of the bird and feels himself a part of that life.

These are rare moments, but they are probably the periods of preparation for the light that ultimately awaits every spiritual student. This is the most sacred experience an individual can ever know: the love of God flowing without limit or hindrance, the love we feel for God, which is God's love flowing through us.

When we recognize the omnipresent Love, a whole new dimension of life opens to us, and we realize:

My only desire is to live consciously in Thy presence. All other desires I surrender unto Thee. Nothing is greater than my love for Thee and my realization of what the government of Thy love and wisdom means.

Here I am, inside myself, alone with Thee, tabernacling with Thee, living in the Kingdom within, and looking only to this deep withinness, this deep pool of contentment within myself for whatever it is that Thou hast to impart to me.

Here within me Thou hast placed Thy beloved son, and this Son is the reality of my being. Deep down within me is Thy presence, and in Thy presence is fullness of life.

Thy presence within me is infinite love. Where Thou art, only love can be expressed. Where Thou art, only wisdom can be expressed. Where Thou art, only peace can be known. And Thou art within me.

Together, communing with one another, Thou hast made my consciousness Thy dwelling place. Thy presence is the activity of divine Grace, and Thy grace is my sufficiency in all things. I can do all things through Thy presence within me, the presence of Thine all-embracing love. Thy love is a law of life unto me, and every demand made upon me is fulfilled by Thine omnipresent love.

If I am healthy, this is an evidence of Thy presence within me. If I have abundance, this is an evidence of Thy presence within me. If I have joy, peace, and harmony, these, too, bear witness to Thy presence of love within me. If I serve, if I help, if I benefit anyone, this is the testimony of Thy love consciously realized.

Thy love! I feel It. It is here within me. It goes before me; It walks beside me, behind me, and always It looks over my shoulder showing me which way to go. Held in Thy love, I walk uprightly and confidently.

~ 5 ~

THE
SPIRITUAL
BOND

Between God and His creation there exists only a relationship of love, a love that truly binds, a love that unites God and man in an eternal relationship of oneness. When a man and a woman acknowledge the inseparable and indivisible bond of oneness existing between them and the Father, that automatically creates a bond between them.

Only a spiritual bond existing between a man and a woman can keep them forever in love and keep that love fruitful, fulfilling, harmonious, and pure. Such a bond comes about when a person can look his partner in the eye and know that here is someone he can trust. This kind of trust makes for lasting peace and a sense of absolute completeness.

In such a spiritual relationship, all sensuality, lust, and greed drop away because this bond establishes them in the household of God, of the family of God. Between them, then, there can be only the pure and unselfish relationship that exists between God and his children and between all the children of the household of God. If they can look upon one another in that light, because of the one Father, the one Life, and one Spirit, the one Soul, automatically and instantaneously, an indestructible bond is created between them. They have seen the Father shining out through the eyes of the members of their family and that makes it impossible to lie, cheat, or defraud any one of them.

No person can be joined by a spiritual bond with another and live with him or her in any other way than that of peace, purity, harmony, completeness, and sharing. What happens then in this senseless human universe cannot possibly make any difference! The insanity of mankind might be recognized but it would never interfere with the relationship established with those of a person's spiritual household.

Human differences become of no moment or have no effect. Where there is love what arguments or problems come up can always be worked out and a solution found without consulting outsiders or going to court. Only when there is an absence of love do arguments have to be settled arbitrarily by an outside party.

In the recognition of the one Father and in the realization of our spiritual bond, we not only have established our oneness with God but our oneness with one another. It is here that a miracle takes place that can never be accounted for in any human way. When we realize our oneness with God and that whatever we are is but an expression of the qualities of God working in and through us, that we of ourselves have no qualities, but by virtue of our oneness with God all the qualities of God can be made manifest through us, then without knowing how or why, our relationship with others is established with their spiritual identity and with ours.

What difference if we are twenty thousand miles away and neither one of us has ever heard of the other! It is inevitable that we will meet. We are not only going to meet: we are going to meet in a joyous, fruitful, and beneficial way because through our conscious contact

with the Father we have been given contact
with all those who are a part of our household
and of whose household we may be a part. In
this realization we have made contact with
everybody and with everything necessary to
play a part in our experience here on earth.
Some we may not meet for five or more years
from now, but at the moment when they fit
into the scheme of our experience there will be
a meeting. We will never lack for the person or
the condition necessary to our harmonious
unfoldment.

We have made ourselves one with every
person and with everything necessary in our
experience the moment we have established a
spiritual bond with God. In making that spiritual bond with God, we have established a
bond with all spiritual being, whether a blade
of grass, a garden, a home, employment, or
whatever will result in fulfilling our experience
on earth.

Love is what binds us together. And what is love? Love is the ability of the Christ in me to speak to the Christ in you. Love is the ability of the Christ in me to recognize and bear witness to the Christ in you. Love is the ability to know that God is just as much your life as He is my life. Love is the ability to recognize that God's grace is bestowed upon you as well as upon me. Every truth that I know about me is the truth I know about you, and that is how I love you—by knowing God's truth about you. You feel it; you respond to it.

~6~

A

WEDDING

TALK*

Human marriage itself, as we know it today, is not too successful, but it would be unnatural for it to be successful as it is known today because it is said that in marriage two become one, and that has been interpreted

---

*From *The Spiritual Journey of Joel S. Goldsmith* by Lorraine Sinkler.

to mean that one or the other loses his identity and individuality; the wife even loses her name.

Two becoming one does not mean the separation or the loss of individual identity or individuality, for this is an utter impossibility. An individual remains an individual, not only from birth to death, but actually long before birth until long, long after death. We never lose our individuality; we never lose our uniqueness. It is an impossibility for an individual to give up, to surrender, or to lose that which constitutes his being, and human marriage tries to make either the man or the woman submit himself or herself and surrender that which is most precious in the sight of God: his or her individual expression of God being. Each of us is individual, each of us has individual qualities, each of us has individual talents and gifts, and these are not to be surrendered in marriage. . . .

In a spiritual marriage there is not bondage but freedom, but this is not true in human marriage. It is true in spiritual marriage, where both recognize that in marrying they are setting each other free. This is the only thing I have discovered in thirty years of this work that will make possible happy marriages, peaceful marriages, successful marriages: the ability to set the other free that each may live his own individual life, and yet share with each other without demanding.

In human marriage a husband has certain rights and a wife has certain rights, but in a spiritual marriage this is not true. Neither husband nor wife has any rights: they have only the privilege of loving; they have only the privilege of sharing. They have the privilege of giving, but they have no right to demand anything of the other. We do not leave human experience while we hold someone in bondage to our rights.

In marriage in the human world, a husband undertakes the support of a wife. Spiritually a wife never expects this, because it would be giving up her God-given heritage of maintaining in consciousness her union with God, in which she finds her supply. When she does, the husband is free to share, without the bondage of being legally compelled to do something. None of us likes to do anything under compulsion, whether legal compulsion or moral compulsion, but we all enjoy the freedom of giving. This is natural. No wife feels honored in being called upon to fulfill a duty or obligation, but every woman must feel, as does every man, the great joy of giving and sharing spontaneously, when it is permitted to be through free will—an offering of the heart, not of the law court.

The return of the Prodigal to the Father's house is the mystical marriage. When an individual under the sense of separation from

God becomes reunited in Spirit and finds in the relationship conscious union with God, this is termed the mystical marriage. Man separated from his Source is never complete.

On the other hand, when an individual finds conscious oneness with God, he finds oneness with all spiritual being and idea, and this includes every relationship in heaven and on earth. Therefore, marriage on the human plane is really the consummation of mystical marriage, conscious union with God. Without conscious union with God, no human marriage can endure, because it is not true that in union there is strength, except that in union with God there is strength. When we then, individually, man and woman, make our conscious contact with God, we have made our conscious union with our husband or wife, with our children, with our neighbors, with our nation, and with the nations of the world. There is no such thing as strength in union unless the relationship first is union with God. Then we are strengthened in our union with each other on every level of human society.

Let no one believe that a marriage is a permanent institution which has not first been experienced by both the husband and wife in their conscious union with God. Then this makes a union between them that is impossible to break. Sometimes it is said in the marriage ceremony that what God has joined together, let no man put asunder. But of course this is impossible. What God has joined together, no man *can* put asunder. It is an indestructible relationship, that which God has cemented, that which God has united; but there is no unitedness, there is no union except in conscious union with God.

If I may say this to you from personal experience, discords have no way of entering the home or the marriage of the couple who unite in meditation frequently. If the life of the

spiritual world, of spiritual activity, has taught
me anything, it is this: where we unite in
meditation, love develops. There is the love
between teacher and student, which is indestructible. There is the love between students
which is indestructible. There is the love
between man and wife which is closer than
any relationship imaginable. There is the
relationship between parents and children
which is something not understood in this
world, because it is not of this world.

A marriage, then, which is not to be a
marriage of this world but is to be a marriage
of *My** kingdom, the spiritual kingdom, a
marriage that is not to have the peace that the
world can give but is to have *My* peace, must
be a marriage that is not only united in spirit,
but one in which the union is maintained by
constant meditation, in which we unite with
God and with each other.

My, capitalized, refers to God

44 THE GIFT OF LOVE

This is the secret of meditation. In meditation we unite with God, and in uniting with God, we find ourselves united with all mankind receptive and responsive to the spiritual urge. More so is this true in marriage. In uniting with God, especially where man and wife together unite with God, they find a union or unitedness between themselves which is indestructible, because it is much more than a personal relationship. It rises above even the good of human relationships. It dissolves all that is evil in human relationships. It dissolves all that is sensual, all that is jealous, all that is malicious, all that is demanding, and it becomes the free-will gift of God to us, and the free-will gift of God to each other.

There is no such thing as a question that can come into a home that cannot be solved by united meditation when each enters it, not for the purpose of gaining his will, wish, or desire, but rather of surrendering his will, wish, or desire, so that the will of God may be made evident. This is the secret, and there is no other. Human relationships on every level of life can be harmoniously maintained only, however, in the surrender of our will to God, not in the surrender of our individuality to each other.

Let us always honor and respect the individuality of the other. Let us remember that no two people have grown from childhood to maturity without developing individual traits of character, of habit, of living, and let us never believe they can surrender these just because they have entered into marriage. Therefore, even sometimes when the ways, the modes, the means of our partner are not completely that of ourselves, let us forget that. In giving them their freedom to be themselves, and as long as they "be themselves" in union with God, marriage is an indestructible relationship on earth as it is in heaven.

~ 7 ~

CHILDREN
OF A
SPIRITUAL UNION

A man and a woman who marry with the enlightened attitude that the children born to them have a higher destiny than to be born of the flesh alone are recognizing the spiritual truth that God is to appear on earth in another form, that another son of God is to come into expression, not their child, not somebody who looks like them, but somebody who looks like God and acts like God.

When two persons unite in marriage in that realization, their children will be born into their Christhood because before conception the parents will know that their coming together is just their part in giving the child visible expression, but will also recognize that no man on earth is its true father and no woman on earth is its true mother.

There is but one Father, God; and God is the creator, the maintainer, and sustainer of all. Parents are but the instruments through which God's grace expressed as individual being comes to earth. God is the child's Father and Mother, his creative Principle. Therefore, all that God is and shows forth will become the nature of the child.

Once the Spirit of God is universally recognized, there will be a different breed of children brought forth on earth. Children then will show forth not the glory of their human but of their divine parentage, manifested as the grace and capacity of that divine Parent.

~8~

How to
Express Love
to Your Family

You will know real peace and love in your household only when you tabernacle and commune with the Spirit of God in man. The way is straight and narrow, and few there are who are willing to engage in the practice necessary to attain a consciousness of that Spirit.

If you expect a man or a woman to be good, or if you are looking to anyone for honesty, you can be mistaken and disappointed time after time. Furthermore, if you are looking at honest men and women and neglecting to see the Christ in each one, do not think for a minute that here and there one of them is not going to trip you up. If, however, in all your human relationships, you insist on looking through every person to the Spirit of God in him, you will be protected from the evil ones of this world, and none of the weapons that are formed against you will prosper.

In the moment that the Spirit of God enters your soul, you see with different eyes, and you lose all sense of male, female, young, old, sick, or well. You see the spiritual identity of all with whom you come in contact and that vision awakens it in them.

In your real identity you are the son of God, but this sonship is so dormant in your humanhood that you have lost the awareness and the capacity to behold the Christ in the members of your family. As you attain spiritual discernment and look out and behold the Christ of them, their capacity to sin or to be sick is diminished.

Take a five-minute period every day in which you meditate for a different member of your family. Begin with your husband, your wife, one of your children, or one of your parents, but take a different person each day for just five, six, or seven minutes. Wait until you are completely free from other responsibilities so that you can go off into a room by yourself without interruptions from the telephone, radio, television, or guests.

Whether the person you have in mind is aware of it or not, you realize that that *I*, that Spirit of God, is already within him, not outside of him, but within him. Know that the Christ is knocking at the door of his consciousness for recognition: "Now I see the son of God, the Spirit of God within you. I pay no

attention to your humanhood or to what degree of goodness or badness you show forth,
what degree of sickness or health, or what
degree of ignorance or wisdom. For this minute I am ignoring all that, because now I am
beholding the Spirit of God in you. I am lifting
up the Christ of God in you, raising up the son
of God out of the tomb of your humanhood."

Most of you are so accustomed to loving
your children in a purely human way that
when you try to ignore their humanhood and
behold the Spirit of God in them, it is almost
as if someone were asking you to stop loving
your child. But for the time being you are
called upon to look right through the child and
say, "I know that in the midst of you is the
child of God and that the Spirit of God in-
dwells you." If you work with that idea day
after day for five minutes at a time, sooner or
later, you will make contact with the Spirit of
God in your child.

The next day take another member of your family and, in this way, go through the entire family whether near or far. If you like, take in some of your friends, or all of them. But remember that you are never going to experience peace on earth with human beings because each one has a selfhood that is trying to preserve itself even at your expense. Peace comes only when every member of your household is recognized as the son of God.

~9~

UPHOLDING
YOUR
LOVED ONES
SPIRITUALLY

It is natural for you to want to place those you love in God's care and, as a matter of fact, unless this is consciously done by someone, your loved ones will not be in God's care. So each day realize the activity of the presence of God and then wait for God to place the seal on your meditation:

*"Whither shall I flee from thy presence?"
Whither shall those of my household flee from Thy
presence? Thy presence fills all space. Thy kingdom
is within the very consciousness of those of my
household, and God is dwelling in His kingdom.*

*Every person in this household is the abiding
place of God; his mind is the temple of God; his
body is the temple of God; and God is in His
dwelling place now. The Spirit of God is the very
breath of his being, the very life of his body, and the
very intelligence of his mind. God envelops him for
God is in him and he is in God.*

*In God's presence is fullness of life, and every
individual in this household, being always in the
presence of God, is always in the presence of the
fullness of life. The place whereon he stands is holy
ground. He and his heavenly Father are one and
inseparable, indivisible, and he cannot stray from
God's presence whether at work or at home. God*

walks with him and as him; God talks with him and as him.

~ 10 ~

LOVE
SEEKETH NOT
HER OWN

❧

Love has in it no desire for return or recompense, so if what you do has in it any desire for reward, recognition, or gratitude, it becomes trade, not love.

When two persons who say they love each other take the attitude, "You do this, and I'll do that," that is not love. That is trade. Love is what a person feels and does without a single trace of hope or desire for reward.

The best way to explain it is to think of what
you do for your children. You certainly have
no thought of doing for them, hoping for their
gratitude. No, you do for your children because that is your function as parents.

If you could extend that same attitude to all,
you might very well find you would wipe all
discord out of your human relationships. Does
not the discord come because you expect
something in return for what you do? In that
expectation you are violating spiritual law.

Everything that you are entitled to in life
must come from God, not from man—everything. It should be your privilege and joy to do
every job that is given you to the best of your
ability, not for the reward, not for recognition,
not for gratitude, but because the job is to be
done, and the only way you can fulfill yourself
is to do it to the best of your ability.

Your reward, your compensation, and your
life's harmony come from God, not from man.

So if anyone withholds gratitude, recognition, or reward, he is not cheating you. He is cheating himself. Gratitude is one of the great attributes of love, and a person who is not filled with gratitude is devoid of love which means that he is devoid of God. A person who is not grateful, is not cooperative, or who does not share is never cheating the other person. He is cheating only himself.

As far as you and I are concerned, what we do should be done for the fulfillment of God as ourselves. An employee who goes into his place of business, forgets about the boss, forgets about the amount of his salary, and does his job to the utmost of his capacity is soon found to be an invaluable employee and is given his reward. If it does not come in that business, it will be in some other, because if his present employer is not able to appreciate his ability and the service he is giving, some other employer will recognize his capabilities and

quickly take him into his business. The point is
that no one should ever go to a job and work
merely in the hope of a reward because his
reward may not come from that direction.

Just as in business so in the home, no one
should do things just for praise or gratitude,
but because it is his job, and he should do it to
the best of his ability, trusting that reward and
recognition will come from God, not from
man. Harmonious relationships can be maintained only on that basis. If you put into each
relationship what is its due, harmony is bound
to follow.

Love can be summed up as that feeling or
emotion that operates without any desire or
expectancy of a return. It is the free-will giving
of oneself.

The nearest thing to real love is mother
love. That is why mother love, when it is not
selfish love but is true mother love, is the
nearest thing to God love, because the true

mother love is a continuous pouring of itself out to the child, without any thought of a return. It is just "I love to clothe you; I love to feed you; I love to educate you; I love to give the best to you."

The parent never thinks about a return. True, much parental love is selfish love, but I am not speaking of that. I am speaking of parental love in its truest sense, where the parent has no idea in mind except to be a parent, and that means doing and loving to do with no thought of return.

Divine love is that outpouring that asks no return and seeks no reward. When you have it, people can love you, and you can have satisfying relationships with them. They know you are not seeking anything from them. Their mental barriers go down. They feel that you are not trying to take something from them or get something from them. In that sense, they feel this love and confidence and trust, just as a child feels love and confidence and trust in those around him because he knows they are not seeking anything from him.

If you and I were to act toward each other with the knowledge that there is an invisible Presence and Power that knows everything we are doing and everything we are thinking, we would always look to It instead of to each other. In fact, one of the major principles of spiritual living is that we really are never doing anything for each other. We are not do-gooders in the sense that we want to do some good for you. We are doing good only in order to fulfill our relationship to God.

When I was in the business world, I had the feeling that I owed it to myself to do the best job I could do up to my highest understanding at the moment. Later I came into healing work because I thought that there must be a way to remove sin, disease, and death from the earth. That is what has animated me all this time. If anyone receives benefit from my efforts it is not because I have thought about benefiting a person, but because my entire aim has been to remove sin, disease, and death from the earth, and I do not care who gets the benefit from it.

Always of paramount importance to me is: Are there principles that will eliminate from this earth its troubles? Yes, there are, and one of them is that most of the things people hate and fear have no real power. So the first thing to do is to stop hating and fearing what the world calls evil things.

The second principle that will remove troubles from the world is love, not the kind of love that seeks a personal return, but the kind of love that seeks to express its own integrity. We all know that sculptors or musicians do not think of buyers or audiences; I mean, the real ones. All they think of is fulfilling themselves and bringing their best to light. When you are willing to let the love and gratitude of God flow through you, with no hope of a return, then you are beginning to know what love is, and that love is the cement that establishes harmony in a business as well as in a home, and eventually in our government.

It is pointless to try to find a reason for loving. Love has no relationship to a reason. If you need a reason, it is not love. Real love operates without reason, beyond reason.

All human relationships must be based on love, but love must be understood as the outpouring of that which seeks no return. Then and only then is it love; then and only then does it result in harmonious relationships.

~ 11 ~

BE
A TRANSPARENCY
FOR LOVE

G od's gifts are given unto all of us imper-
sonally and wholly without favoritism;
there is no provision in the kingdom of God
for leaving anyone outside of His love and
grace. If we find ourselves outside of that
Grace, it is not God's fault but ours. We have
not been disinherited or disowned: we have
simply withdrawn ourselves from Grace.
Whatever is of God is meant for the sons of

God, and only when we claim something that is God's for ourselves personally do we lose it; but when we claim God's glory as the universal gift of God to his children we all partake of it.

As we begin to live in this way, we are not trying to mold God to our will; we are not trying to make God do something for us: we are yielding ourselves to God's love; we are surrendering ourselves to God's will.

Freedom, justice, liberty, abundance, health, youth, and vitality—all these are the gifts of God, and they are included in that Love which is without price; they are all for His glory that it may be made evident to man on earth as it is in heaven.

Our homes should be centers of love, instead of places where criticism, judgment, condemnation, lack of understanding, and lack of cooperation are harbored. For those on the spiritual path, home should be the temple of God:

This is Thy home, Father. This is Thy abiding place. Fill every corner of it with Thy presence; let love reign here.

Let my consciousness be devoid of human emotions, negative feelings and actions, and let me be an instrument through which Thy presence finds entrance into this home.

As we realize more and more that our function in our household is to be the instrument through which God is to find entrance, we purge our consciousness of its human qualities; we learn to forgive injustices quickly and to forget offenses, realizing that God neither judges nor condemns, and that neither must we. God's forgiveness is seventy times unto seven and so must ours be. Not only must we express love, patience, kindness, justice, cooperation, and generosity in our home, but we must love our neighbors as ourselves. Then does our consciousness become a transparency through which God's love enters and blesses the multitudes.

Regardless of where we live or work, or where we function on the human plane, let us remember that God does not enter into that activity except through a consciousness that is a transparency for God, that is willing consciously to let itself be used that God may find entrance. This demands daily practice:

My consciousness, which has in it nothing but love, which has no desire for gain and no desire for glory, is now a transparency through which God is flowing into this world. Because God cannot be limited in time or space, or by walls, the realized presence of God in this room is flowing out of this room, up and down the street, up and down the nation, and across the waters.

I am an instrument and a transparency through which God's love blesses mankind—friend and foe. My consciousness does not condemn the sinner; my

*consciousness does not seek vengeance, but forgive-
ness. Through my consciousness of love, God enters
my home, my business, my nation, and this whole
universe.*

If we give the love of God just a tiny crack
through which to enter this world, we shall see
how quickly that love will encircle the
globe–faster than sound, faster than light. But
there must be an entrance made into this
world for God, or else God is kept outside.

If there are "ten" righteous men in the city,
the city will be saved, and if there are groups
dotting this earth, praying the prayer of the
righteous, the whole world can be saved. Let
all those on the spiritual path pray daily:

*I am not in this world to acquire or achieve
anything: I am here as an instrument of God to bear
witness to God's presence. I was born only for one
reason, that God, through me, may be made manifest on earth. I was born for the glory of God, not for*

my personal glory, not for my personal reputation or my personal wealth, but born that God might be glorified as His love is shown forth through me.

We become transparencies for God when we dedicate ourselves to loving God and to loving our neighbor as ourselves. This dedication of our consciousness need take only a few minutes, but it should be repeated at least two or three times a day:

In the name of the Father, peace; be still.
I bring no condemnation into this world. Because of my love for God and for my neighbor, may love flow through my consciousness and bless and forgive and uplift and free mankind—my enemy and my friend, that they may be free of lust and greed and hate and fear and doubt. May God's love touch their consciousness and awaken their souls.

Our consciousness must be the transparency whereby God's love can find entrance to the earth and God's reign can take place on earth as it is in heaven. Every consciousness that is dedicated to the love of God and the love of neighbor becomes an open window through which the light of truth, love, and life enters this world, dispelling the darkness and establishing the reign of God on earth as it is in heaven.

God's presence must be consciously admitted into this world: a window must be opened; shades must be lifted so that the light of love can enter. But if God's love is not entering through the window of our consciousness, it is because our consciousness is soiled, soiled with the only kind of dirt that can soil it, a dirt that is spelled s-e-l-f, I, me, and mine.

When we begin to cleanse our consciousness, when we begin to realize less and less of self, and more and more of love, more and more of forgiveness, more and more of praise, glory, and gratitude, more and more of a willingness for God to touch the consciousness of the sinner, the tyrant, the ignorant, and the atheist, and if we can open one tiny little speck of our consciousness for God to get in, God will so multiply Himself over the face of this earth that it will be literally proved that where "ten" righteous men are, the city will be saved.

Let us acknowledge ourselves to be living witnesses to the presence of God; let us learn to awaken in the morning and, after realizing God's presence, do what is given us to do—whatever it may be—to the best of our ability, and then go on to the next task. Long before we come to the end of all that is awaiting us to do, new tasks will be given us, and with them will come recompense, recognition, and reward, not because we seek them, but because they are the added things.

Let us seek nothing but the opportunity to do the work that is given us to do. If a letter of condolence or a letter of thanks should be written, let us write it now; if a word of praise or gratitude should be spoken, let us express it freely and generously; if a cupboard is to be cleaned, let us clean it now; if there are old clothes to be given away, let us give them away now. Let us do each day the task that is given us to do, regardless of how mundane it may appear to be; and if we fulfill that which is given us to do now, we shall find that more important things, and eventually what appear to be more spiritual things, will be given us to do—but not until we have done that which has already been given us to do.

Our first and foremost task is to fill our consciousness with love, forgiveness, gratitude, praise, loyalty, and devotion, not only to God but to our neighbor as well. We must heal and cleanse ourselves until our consciousness is purged of self, and we become transparencies through which God's love reaches the earth. It is always with ourselves that we have to begin,

and it is always with ourselves that we have to
end.